Keep It Simple, Sweetheart

Attitude Is Everything

The content of this book is almost identical
to the content of
"Keep it Simple"

Anita Elisabeth van den Brink

PROLOGUE

Having worked in leadership in the business world for 15 years and as a board member at a church for 5 years, I have learned a lot. I've learned the most from my mistakes and inabilities. Over the years, I have come to see how the Bible truly has all the answers and what immense blessings it brings when we put the Bible into practice, especially when it seems unfair, simplistic or impossible. God's Word works. In this booklet, I will explore some themes that leaders regularly encounter.

If this booklet encourages you to truly live out the Bible, even when it does not seem to make sense, I will have achieved my goal. And... ssssttt... here's the secret: if you live out the Bible by showing a Biblical attitude in every situation, especially when it is difficult to do so, a peace that surpasses all understanding will be yours.

You will know His favor, His anointing, His joy, His love, His patience, His kindness, His self-control... Who would not want these things?

INTRODUCTION:
THE STORY OF JOSEPH

"....all things work together for good to them that love God..."

(Romans 8:28)

I love the story of Joseph in Genesis 37-50. I encourage you to read his story. If you are looking for examples of injustice, then this story more than fits the bill.

Joseph was his father's favorite. His father gave him, and only him, a beautiful robe. He could have chosen to share his robe with his eleven brothers. He could have asked his father to give a robe to all his brothers; instead, he pranced around in his exquisite new garment. Not the best way to keep the peace with your siblings...

Joseph dreamed vivid dreams. In one of them, he saw his older brothers bowing to him. He cheerfully shared this dream with his brothers. As you can well imagine, this did not endear Joseph to his brothers. To make a long story short, Joseph was tied up and sold into slavery by his brothers. He ended up as a slave to Potiphar, an officer in the court of Pharaoh, the ruler of Egypt.

During his enslavement in the house of Potiphar,

Joseph was falsely accused by Potiphar's wife of trying to seduce her – which was in actual fact what she was trying to do to him. Potiphar believed his wife's lie and had Joseph thrown into jail.

> "But the LORD was with Joseph and showed him steadfast love and gave him favor in the sight of the keeper of the prison. And the keeper of the prison put Joseph in charge of all the prisoners who were in the prison. Whatever was done there, he was the one who did it. The keeper of the prison paid no attention to anything that was in Joseph's charge, because the LORD was with him. And whatever he did, the LORD made it succeed."
>
> (Genesis 39:21-23)

Pharaoh's cupbearer was thrown into jail with him; Joseph helped the man by interpreting his dream. He asked the cupbearer to remember him when he was released... but once the cupbearer was released, he quickly forgot about the person who had helped him in jail.

If we had gone through all of this, by now, I'm guessing most of us would feel like we had every right to be bitter, despondent, deeply disillusioned with life and with people. Not Joseph, though. Joseph was betrayed by his brothers and sold as a slave, falsely accused by Potiphar's wife, forgotten by the cupbearer, sitting out time in prison for a crime that he did not commit.

From what we can tell, Joseph maintained a good attitude. The cupbearer may have forgotten about Joseph, but God did not. Two years later, when Pharaoh had a strange dream, the cupbearer finally remembered him. Joseph was brought before Pharaoh to interpret the dream. Joseph clearly explained that it was God, not he, who would interpret the dream, and proceeded to help Pharaoh by giving him an interpretation.

> "And Pharaoh said to Joseph, 'See, I have set you over all the land of Egypt.' Then Pharaoh took his signet ring from his hand and put it on Joseph's hand, and clothed him in garments of fine linen and put a gold chain about his neck."
>
> (Genesis 41:41-42)

It was a long journey, involving extreme circumstances, but we see that Joseph has developed character along the way. He changed from a proud teenager who perhaps reveled in his father's favoritism, into a man who chose to maintain a good attitude despite betrayal, false witness against him, wrongful incarceration and being forgotten.

> "… in all these things we are more than conquerors
> through him who loved us."
>> (Romans 8:37)

Joseph had every reason to consider himself a victim, yet in all these things he was indeed more than a conqueror.

As it says in James 1:2-4,
> "Consider it pure joy, my brothers and sisters, whenever you face trials of many kinds, because you know that the testing of your faith produces perseverance. Let perseverance finish its work so that you may be mature and complete, not lacking anything."

These verses from James make a lot more sense after reading a story like this one about Joseph's life. We are only halfway, though, so let's continue.

Joseph was now in charge in Egypt, and, knowing through the interpretation of Pharaoh's dream that a famine was coming, he made sure that vast quantities of food were stored up during the time of plenty. He

was obviously a wise manager, planner and leader.
When the time of famine came, Joseph was able to supply all those in need. Soon his own family was in need too – and this is when it gets interesting. What would Joseph do to the brothers who sold him, who did not care about or for him? What would he do when they turned to him in their time of need?

Many of us would say that Joseph had every right to turn them away. To give them a piece of his mind, and not a pretty piece; to show off his new status and to send them back empty-handed, making sure that they deeply regretted their bad behavior in the past.
But that was not what he did. He tested them in several ways. In the end, he revealed who he was, wept uncontrollably and proceeded to bless them abundantly by providing them with what they needed.

In Genesis 50:20, Joseph says to his brothers,
> "*As for you, you meant evil against me, but God meant it for good...*".

What a powerful statement! The story goes on to say:
> "*Thus he comforted them and spoke kindly to them.*"
> (Genesis 50:21b)

I wonder, how kindly would you and I speak to those who envied us, betrayed us and sold us off?

The fascinating thing about this story is that all the injustices, both the unfair things Joseph did in his youth and the injustices committed against him, caused Joseph to develop a Godly character. This inner growth in turn caused him to be put in a position of great power, thus enabling him to bless his family abundantly in their time of need. Joseph was only able to bless his brothers because he first forgave them.

Now, how about us?
How can we ensure that God's purposes are fulfilled in our lives?
How do we allow God to transform our negative situations into a life, filled with victory?
How do we maintain peace when everyone, especially those whom we should have been able to trust, turns against us?
Read on!

INJUSTICE
VERSUS JUSTICE

Have you been treated unfairly? Felt overlooked at work, perhaps? You've given your all and no one seems to notice? A colleague got that promotion that you felt you deserved? Your parents favored your gifted sibling? Or perhaps your parents favored your disadvantaged sibling, and left you to your own devices? Your spouse never seems to notice you? You addressed an issue with someone and he turned against you? You've given your child everything, and now your child is rebellious and rejects you? People have been slandering you and no one is doing anything about it?

My guess is that we all face injustice in life, some to a lesser degree and others more so. The question is, how do we respond to the injustices? How do we steer clear of a victim mentality? How do we become victors instead of victims?

Romans 12:9-21 gives us a great summary of how to deal with these things. We can see many of these attitudes reflected in Joseph's choices:

> *"Love must be sincere. Hate what is evil; cling to what is good. Be devoted to one another in love.*

Honor one another above yourselves. Never be
lacking in zeal, but keep your spiritual fervor,
serving the Lord. Be joyful in hope, patient in
affliction, faithful in prayer. Share with the Lord's
people who are in need. Practice hospitality.
Bless those who persecute you; bless and do not curse.
Rejoice with those who rejoice; mourn with those
who mourn. Live in harmony with one another.
Do not be proud, but be willing to associate with
people of low position. Do not be conceited.
Do not repay anyone evil for evil. Be careful to do
what is right in the eyes of everyone. If it is possible,
as far as it depends on you, live at peace with
everyone. Do not take revenge, my dear friends, but
leave room for God's wrath, for it is written: 'It is
mine to avenge; I will repay,' says the Lord. On the
contrary:
'If your enemy is hungry, feed him; if he is thirsty, give
him something to drink. In doing this, you will heap
burning coals on his head.' Do not be overcome by evil,
but overcome evil with good."

I don't know about you, but much of this does not
come naturally to me. In fact, my natural response
would probably be quite the opposite of what Romans
12:9-21 says and... having been in leadership for many
years, I have seen that I am not the only one.

How do we live according to Romans 12? How can we be "patient in affliction", "bless those who persecute us" and "overcome evil with good"?

Can we ever do that relying on our own strength? All I can say is that I need God, His Holy Spirit, to transform me into responding His way. I need His Word to transform me. I need to choose to obey His Word and to practice the fruits of the Spirit that He has already instilled in you and me.

In the coming chapters, I will briefly explore some pitfalls that we might fall into when we experience times of trial.

ANGER
VERSUS FORGIVENESS

Injustice can cause us to feel hurt. If we are hurt, getting angry is one possible natural response. Anger is often a secondary emotion; the deeper layer could be disappointment, pain, sadness, grief, fear, a feeling of betrayal or many other emotions. It helps to recognize the deeper emotion and to express that emotion to God and to the person who triggered the emotional response, rather than expressing your anger.

The Bible does not condemn anger as such. Instead, it says:

> "*In your anger do not sin*", adding: "*Do not let the sun go down while you are still angry*".
> (Ephesians 4:26)

This is a clear command to deal with our anger within one day. Ideally, we would deal with it by resolving the problem the same day, but that is not always possible. Sometimes we need to deal with our anger, our feeling of being offended, even when the issue has not been resolved yet.

How do we do that? It starts with humility. It starts with a deep conviction that we too are sinners and
"*fall short of the glory of God*".
(Romans 3:23)

In Genesis 45, we see Joseph make himself known to his brothers. He effectively extended forgiveness to his brothers before they had even asked for forgiveness for their sin against him.

"*I am your brother Joseph, the one you sold into Egypt! And now, do not be distressed and do not be angry with yourselves for selling me here, because it was to save lives that God sent me ahead of you.*"
(Genesis 45:4b-5)

How powerful. The devil would have loved to have Joseph be bitter and unforgiving toward his brothers. That was probably the design of the evil one. Joseph broke that design by returning good for evil, and forgiving despite not having heard his brothers apologize. This can be tough and can seem deeply unjust, yet we are doing others a favor in doing so – and are benefiting ourselves as well. When we choose to forgive even though the offender has not taken responsibility for his or her role, we walk the path of freedom and... we extend the same forgiveness to him that God has extended to us.

So, in humility we can choose to forgive; we can pray, "Father, I forgive such and such, as you have forgiven me for all of my sins". This is a choice, not a feeling. Your feelings will follow, sometimes soon, but perhaps much, much later. But God will honor your choice.

How God blesses us by reminding us not to let the sun go down while we are still angry. God knows how quickly our hearts grow bitter, and out of bitterness we behave like powerless victims. When we are bitter, we respond like hurt people. When people feel hurt... they proceed to hurt others themselves.

If you need humility to choose forgiveness, I submit to you that you need pride to stay offended.

"How dare you to do this to me?" What we are implying is, "How dare you treat perfect, wonderful me this way?"

> *"The pride of your heart has deceived you."*
> (Obadiah 1:3a)

> *"The proud one shall stumble and fall."*
> (Jeremiah 50:32a)

If we truly understand our own humanity, our own fallibility and therefore our own desperate need for God's forgiveness, which He freely and lovingly extends to us, forgiving others becomes a lot easier.

It must have taken a lot of humility for Joseph to treat his brothers well. He could have chosen offense, pride and bitterness. If Joseph had done so, he would not have blessed his brothers. If that had happened, his brothers would not have received the food that they needed in a time of need, his family might have starved, and Joseph would have been known for returning evil for evil. Instead, Joseph chose to overcome evil with good.

JUDGING VERSUS BLESSING

If we perceive an offense, we can easily turn to judgment, slander and gossip. If injustice is done to us, let us guard our tongues. The Bible is full of verses about the tongue. Here are a few:

> *"Whoever keeps his mouth and his tongue keeps himself out of trouble."*
>
> (Proverbs 21:23)

> *"Let no corrupting talk come out of your mouths, but only such as is good for building up, as fits the occasion, that it may give grace to those who hear."*
>
> (Ephesians 4:29)

> *"There is one whose rash words are like sword thrusts, but the tongue of the wise brings healing."*
>
> (Proverbs 12:18)

> *"If anyone thinks he is religious and does not bridle his tongue but deceives his heart, this person's religion is worthless."*
>
> (James 1:26)

"Death and life are in the power of the tongue, and those who love it will eat its fruits."

(Proverbs 18:21)

"When words are many, transgression is not lacking, but whoever restrains his lips is prudent."

(Proverbs 10:19)

It can be a major trial to keep our mouths shut when someone has deeply offended us and another person speaks well of him, and... even more difficult to then smile and speak kindly of the offender. Yet... if you choose to bless those who persecute you, you will have peace in your heart and in the end, you will overcome evil with good.

In his later years, Joseph was a brilliant example of this. Right before he revealed himself to his brothers, he asked everyone who was not related to him to leave the room.

"Then Joseph could no longer control himself before all his attendants, and he cried out, 'Have everyone leave my presence!' So there was no one with Joseph when he made himself known to his brothers. And he wept so loudly that the Egyptians heard him, and Pharaoh's household heard about it."

(Genesis 45:1-2)

Joseph does not blemish the name and reputation of his brothers to anyone outside his family. In fact, as far as I can tell, he does not even 'tattle' on his brothers to their father. That is mercy. That is forgiveness.

I submit to you that we should speak *to* each other and not *about* each other. This means that if someone comes to me to speak about another person whom he has been hurt by or feels offended by, I should address the person speaking to me and help that person in his attitude, his choices and his actions. I should not make it about the person who is not present.

As a young leader, I soon learned that offended people would often tell the truth, but they would often leave out their own part, perhaps 20% of the story. This 20% of the story that they had left out was often key to bringing restoration. I have been astounded at people's capacity to take insult at a word thrown at them and, upon asking them what they said or did to the other party just before the word was spoken, discovering that he had been just as insulting in *their* words or deeds.

> "He who states his case first seems right, until his rival comes and cross-examines him."
>   (Proverbs 18:17)

Seeing this in others makes me wonder how easily I might fall into the same trap.

We sure do love to look at our own motives and actions from a perspective of great grace, yet when someone else does something to us, we can be harsh and condemning. Let's practice the same grace towards others that we love to give ourselves.

Judgment

> *"Judge not, that you be not judged. For with the judgment you pronounce you will be judged, and with the measure you use it will be measured to you. Why do you see the speck that is in your brother's eye, but do not notice the log that is in your own eye? Or how can you say to your brother, 'Let me take the speck out of your eye,' when there is the log in your own eye? You hypocrite, first take the log out of your own eye, and then you will see clearly to take the speck out of your brother's eye."*
> (Matthew 7:1-5)

I absolutely love these verses. I have caught myself inwardly starting to pick on someone else's speck, completely ignoring the log in my own eye.
It can be deeply troubling to see people judge others

for things that they themselves are doing and even more troubling if the person with the log in his eye takes great insult if he is admonished.

> "...But who are you to judge your neighbor?"
> (James 4:12)

We are not supposed to judge others. Judgment is up to God and God only. We can let someone know that we do not appreciate his behavior, but to judge someone's motives, or even our own, is a different matter. I submit to you that judgment is not up to us. Our hearts can deceive us. I could easily overestimate my own motives or, if I have a tendency to condemn myself, I might underestimate my motives. I suggest that we are to leave judgment to God and simply address behavior, not motives.

Notice the words;
> "Judge not, and you will not be judged; condemn not, and you will not be condemned; forgive, and you will be forgiven."
> (Luke 6:37)

I believe that calling each other names is the same as passing judgment on them. This includes statements like, "this person is a hypocrite", "that person is a narcissist", "you are a betrayer". I suggest that we need to steer clear of such statements. Rather, if you are speaking to the person, express your feelings, e.g.: "I feel betrayed."

In the story in Genesis, Joseph had every reason to judge his brothers and call them names. How powerful that, instead, he shed his tears (for his grief was very real) and proceeded to steer clear of judgment. He chose to bless them instead.

I am betrayed!   You feel betrayed.

We need to steer clear of statements.

REBELLION
VERSUS SUBMISSION

"In all your ways submit to him, and he will make your paths straight."

(Proverbs 3:6)

To some of us in the Western world, the idea of submitting to God is perhaps still okay with us. God is the Almighty, fair enough, I can submit to Him...
But then comes this verse:

"Submit yourselves for the Lord's sake to every human authority: whether to the emperor, as the supreme authority, or to governors..."

(1 Peter 2:13-14a)

We prefer to think that it says:
"Submit to every human authority as long as they treat you well..."
Or:
"Submit to every human authority as long as you agree with them..."
Or:
"Submit to every human authority as long as you feel so inclined..."

Or perhaps:

"Submit to every human authority as long *they* do as *you* tell them..."

Do you recognize yourself in any of these attitudes? Well, the truth is, it simply says, "Submit to every human authority". There are no conditions imposed on such submission.

And concerning those who are your leaders in the Lord's work, it says;

> *"And now, friends, we ask you to honor those leaders who work so hard for you, who have been given the responsibility of urging and guiding you along in your obedience. Overwhelm them with appreciation and love!"*
>
> (1 Thessalonians 5:12-13 The Message)

How does that work, you may ask? How do I submit to authority? How do I overwhelm my Christian leaders with love? We all know that human authority is fallible. I know, because I am a fallible authority, and I also serve fallible authorities. Lovely authorities, but still fallible.

Here's the thing: there is great peace and blessing in returning good for evil. In fact, this is so powerful that often, if we consistently return good for evil, as we saw

Joseph do after he was sold into slavery, God can greatly bless us.

My precious readers, do not risk giving up God's purposes for your life by being rebellious to your leaders. Of course there are times when situations require action. When crimes are being committed, when physical abuse is taking place, etc... I am not referring to those kinds of situations.

How do you address an issue with an authority? You gracefully submit the issue to him. Stick to your own story, not to somebody else's. Stick to the facts and explain how they make you feel and what you would like. A fact, a feeling and a desire cannot easily be argued with, so, if you choose to word your issue in this manner, you are more likely to be able to have a healthy dialogue.

If your concerns are not heard or acted upon, let the authority know that you will involve a higher authority. If that does not work, and it is a situation that you believe God does not want you to be in, then gracefully look for another environment and bless the authorities whom you are leaving behind. If your perception of injustice was correct, God will deal with them.

"Brothers, if anyone is caught in any transgression, you who are spiritual should restore him in a spirit of gentleness. Keep watch on yourself, lest you too be tempted. Bear one another's burdens, and so fulfill the law of Christ."

(Galatians 6:1-2)

"If your brother sins against you, go and tell him his fault, between you and him alone. If he listens to you, you have gained your brother. But if he does not listen, take one or two others along with you, that every charge may be established by the evidence of two or three witnesses. If he refuses to listen to them, tell it to the church. And if he refuses to listen even to the church, let him be to you as a Gentile and a tax collector."

(Matthew 18:15-17)

Leaders, be worthy of your position. Address issues: shepherd your flock; love those that God has entrusted to you. You will be held to account.

MOANING & COMPLAINING
VERSUS EXPRESSING GRATITUDE

Joseph could have easily spent his days moaning and groaning about his plight. He had every 'right' to do so. Yet he chose a different attitude.

The Israelites were well known for their complaining.

> "*The Israelites said to them, 'If only we had died by the hand of the Lord in the land of Egypt, when we sat by the fleshpots and ate our fill of bread; for you have brought us out into this wilderness to kill this whole assembly with hunger.'*"
>
> (Exodus 16:3)

Even though the Israelites were free, they were still living in captivity because of their attitudes. Their moaning and complaining showed God that they were not ready for the Promised Land. They were no longer slaves, but they still spoke and behaved like slaves. Therefore, what should have been a journey of only a few days became a 40-year journey.

Does this mean that we cannot express our feelings? Of course we can. Read the Psalms and you will see every type of despair and feeling expressed to God. And that is exactly the point; express your feelings to God, ask Him to speak to you, but steer clear from moaning and complaining to those around you.

Joseph never denied his feelings. He wept when he saw his brothers, yet he chose to bless them.

Practice speaking out blessings over every situation, even the most extreme situations. Bless those who persecute you, bless your enemies, bless and do not curse.

Let's make that practical. Say you have a spouse, a boss, a ministry leader or a parent who consistently does some things that you are not okay with. Not major moral issues, but some things that you could do without. Let's assume that you have tried addressing the issue in all the appropriate ways, so far without result. Choose a different approach; start blessing your spouse, boss, ministry leader, parent by encouraging them in every good thing they do. Thank them for it. Consistently show respect, admiration and appreciation. Not just a week, not just a month, consistently, for a year, for two years if need be.

Try it; you'll be amazed at the effect.

I can almost hear you say: "A year?"

Yes, a year; ten years if need be. Remember what James 1:4 says?

> "*Let perseverance finish its work so that you may be mature and complete, not lacking anything.*"

You and I have a choice: we can live pitiful, powerless lives, or we can live as God intended, and live powerful lives through Him.

You may say, "But that's so difficult." That's right, it is. The Bible never promises us a rose garden. In fact, it promises hardship:

> "*I have told you these things, so that in me you may have peace. In this world you will have trouble. But take heart! I have overcome the world.*"
>
> (John 16:33)

What's more, God would love for us to have a good attitude amidst our trials:

> "*Consider it pure joy, my brothers and sisters, whenever you face trials of many kinds.*"
>
> (James 1:2)

"That's impossible," you may say. You're right, it is impossible. That is precisely why we need God's help. In and of ourselves, most of us cannot live like this. With God, however, all things are possible.

> *"And he said, The things which are impossible with men are possible with God."*
> (Luke 18:27)

Let's remember Joseph's story. What would have happened to Joseph if he had spent his days in prison moaning and complaining? Do you think he would have had time to interpret the dream of the cupbearer? Do you think he would have had the attitude that would instill sufficient trust in Pharaoh to set Joseph "*over all the land of Egypt*"? My best guess is, not so much.

Do yourself and your surroundings a big favor and turn your complaints into a prayer of gratitude and blessing.

STRIFE
VERSUS CONFRONTATION

If you've read all the previous chapters, you may wonder, "Well, if everything is about attitude, does that mean I should never confront an issue but just be a pushover?" Not at all. The point is that your message will be far more effective if you convey it with the right attitude. Confrontation is Biblical. What this world is in desperate need of, are people who confront in a life-giving manner.

What is the right attitude for confrontation? I think we can sum it up with Galatians 5:22-23:

> "But the Spirit produces love, joy, peace, patience, kindness, goodness, faithfulness, humility and self-control. There is no law against such things as these."

Confront someone by kindly and humbly coming alongside him. Patiently explain to him what you have noticed. Keep it factual; tell them what the effect of the fact is on you and what you would like to see happen. If you do all this while recognizing and expressing that you too make plenty of mistakes, and if you keep control over your emotions while speaking, the chances of the person being willing to listen to you will dramatically increase, compared to a confrontation where you speak in anger and judgment.

> *"If it is possible, as far as it depends on you, live at peace with everyone."*
>
> (Romans 12:18)

> *"Have nothing to do with foolish, ignorant controversies; you know that they breed quarrels. And the Lord's servant must not be quarrelsome but kind to everyone, able to teach, patiently enduring evil, correcting his opponents with gentleness. God may perhaps grant them repentance leading to a knowledge of the truth..."*
>
> (2 Timothy 2:23-25)

God hates strife. We have a responsibility to address issues in a godly manner. Having said that, there are times when we have shown a godly attitude, yet peace with someone does not seem possible at that moment. Maintain appropriate boundaries, but keep the door to peace open. Do not shut the door for good, nor should you use definite words like "never", e.g.: "I never want to see you again". Steer clear of such words. Instead, pray a blessing over this person and pray for restoration. In the words of James Bond, "Never say never".

We need to maintain a godly attitude during trouble and confrontation, remembering that God is able to do "*immeasurably more than we pray or ask for.*" (Ephesians 3:20). See how it says in the previous verses in 2 Timothy 2 "*... patiently enduring evil...*". Patience is a fruit of the Spirit, a fruit that we can have and extend, out of Christ's love for that person, a fruit that is so much easier to extend if we practice humility, another fruit of the Spirit.

If you are able, like Joseph, do something good for the person that does not choose a peaceful attitude toward you; bless him abundantly.

Let's remember that if we admonish an abuser and we choose to do so in an abusive way, our words lose their effectiveness. A likely response will be, "Look who's talking!"

Do not let your own behavior turn a confrontation into a conflict. We could easily despair in a difficult situation. Remember to stay very close to God's word. Let His word transform you.

> *"What, then, shall we say in response to these things? If God is for us, who can be against us? He who did not spare his own Son, but gave him up for us all – how will he not also, along with him, graciously give us all things? Who will bring any charge against those whom God has chosen? It is God who justifies. Who*

then is the one who condemns? No one. Christ Jesus
who died – more than that, who was raised to life – is
at the right hand of God and is also interceding for us.
Who shall separate us from the love of Christ? Shall
trouble or hardship or persecution or famine or
nakedness or danger or sword? As it is written: 'For
your sake we face death all day long; we are considered
as sheep to be slaughtered.' No, in all these things we
are more than conquerors through him who loved us."

(Romans 8:31-37)

As it says in Romans, nothing can separate us from the
love of Christ. Not even your own actions. There is no
need to fear. Instead, you can proclaim your trust in
God even when you do not see a positive outcome.
Over the years, I have seen my prayers evolve from
trying to direct God in how He should solve a situation
to simply saying, "Father, may Your will be done in this
situation, may Your purposes be fulfilled". This is a
much more powerful prayer, since God is all-knowing,
while my knowledge is so very limited and can be
clouded by emotions and personal motives.
I find it interesting to study Paul's prayers in the Bible.
I have not caught him praying that a problem would
be taken away. Instead, I see him praying that we
would endure during trials and grow from them. In
today's society, where we love to think that everything

revolves around us, this is quite a revolutionary approach. In fact, I rarely hear anyone preach about standing firm during trials. I often hear how God is our comforter and loves us and takes care of us. All true, but if that is the only part of the Bible that we teach about, we stand a good chance of raising helpless, pitiful Christians. Whereas, from my best understanding of the Bible, the Christian life is a life that calls for and raises up men and women of courage and strength in Him. Who are ready to stand firm in times of trouble are ready for any battle.

Let's keep drawing inspiration from Joseph and his attitude towards his brothers. What would have happened if Joseph had not pursued peace with his brothers? What would have happened if he had given them a piece of his mind, and not a pretty piece at that? What would have happened if Joseph had chosen strife over blessing?
My guess is that his story would have lost all its power; my guess is that Joseph would have literally missed the mark and that Joseph would have missed the purpose that God had for his life. Thankfully Joseph chose another attitude. He chose peace and forgiveness. How about you and I? Are there situations in our lives where we could build a bridge to peace instead of choosing strife?

I am ready to receive feedback!

Let the person avoiding you know
that you would love to receive feedback.

A HARDENED HEART
VERSUS RESTORATION

"It's so weird! This person will not speak to me anymore. I don't understand." This is a situation that I have often seen in my time as a leader. Sometimes, although not always, the person complaining has an overwhelming personality type. In my experience, this often happens to the type of person that speaks accusingly or harshly rather than lovingly, thus distancing people from them. Sadly, these are often the types of people that will readily address issues in others, but will take great offense if an issue is addressed with them, so very few venture to do so.

The only apt advice that I can come up with for the person who is being avoided is: let the person avoiding you know that you would love to receive feedback from him on any issue that he would like to share with you. Let them know that you will listen rather than speak, and that you promise not to take offense now or later. If you do this, you will greatly increase the chance that the person avoiding you will speak to you again.

If you are the 'avoider' and a person that you no longer feel safe with has the courage to approach you and give you this open invitation for feedback, please, be gentle with him, lest you become an abuser yourself.

> *"Having the understanding darkened, being alienated from the life of God through the ignorance that is in them, because of the blindness of their heart."*
>
> (Ephesians 4:18)

It helps, in any difficult relational situation, to remember that our hearts can deceive us:

> *"The heart is deceitful above all things and beyond cure."*
>
> (Jeremiah 17:9)

Please do not overestimate the purity of your own motives. How often do we respond out of the habits that we have learned over the years, yet never questioned? In retrospect, I see so much in my earlier life that I did not question and was clueless about until, through God's Word, I was transformed through the renewing of my mind. How about you? Are you allowing God to transform you, to renew your mind in every situation? I pray that I continue to do so day by day, and I hope the same for you.

May we pray that our hearts remain soft, always, especially during trials of any kind.

FEAR
VERSUS TRUST

I was told that it says "fear not" 365 times in the Bible, one for every day of the year. If this is the case, it tells me that fear is probably a major issue in our lives.

Now, God does not ask us to be without fear. I believe we can recognize and accept our fear and, in Christ's strength, go through the fear and thus overcome it. If we study the previous chapters and look for how much of our natural inclinations in all these circumstances stem from fear, we might be astounded to see how much of our lives, our behavior and our responses are driven by fear.

During trials, we might be tempted to think that the circumstances are there to stay, that the situation is hopeless. That is often our fear. The truth, however, is that there is always hope. I suggest that we can influence a good outcome by our attitude and by our choices in difficult circumstances. We can learn and grow in such a way that a situation that may have caused us great distress in the past can now be a 'piece of cake' to us, no big deal. In Christ, we have overcome it.

It is important to remember that the Bible is not merely a book of do's and don'ts; it is not a book about behavior modification. If I try to change my behavior based solely on my own efforts, I will surely fail. God provides us with the Holy Spirit, who lives in us and can transform our thinking and renew our mind. We need to change from the inside out. In other words, we can change our attitudes and our choices, with Christ's help.

Back to fear versus trust in dealing with issues. Remember that we have the all-powerful God of Heaven and earth on our side. So, if you or I are dealing with, for example, a person in authority, we can do so without fear, because we can trust that God will steer the heart of the person in authority.

> "A king's heart is like streams of water in the LORD's hand: He directs it wherever He chooses."
> (Proverbs 21:1)

Does this mean that the person in authority will always deal with us justly? Not necessarily. Remember the story of Joseph. He was not dealt with justly, but... all the circumstances did lead to the place where God wanted him. Remember this next time that you face an injustice. Choose to trust, instead of responding in fear. If God does not resolve the situation immediately, ask Him to show you what you can learn in the situation, how you can grow and how you can bless those that persecute you. Leave resolving the situation up to God. Believe me, He knows what He is doing. Every story in the Bible proves that.

A weapon, stronger and more powerful than any weapon is: LOVE!

LOVE

Let me share a secret with you: in every difficult situation, there is a weapon that is stronger and more powerful than any weapon you could ever choose to use, and that is LOVE. If you choose to show love in every difficult situation that you face, you will be amazed at what God can do through you.

"But," I hear you say, "it is just so difficult to show love in my situation."

If you study the Bible, it will soon become evident to you that the single most effective way to have peace in your own heart is to spend your time doing good. Love will often beget love. If it doesn't, then at least *you* have peace in *your* heart.

> "*Love is patient, love is kind. It does not envy, it does not boast, it is not proud. It does not dishonor others, it is not self-seeking, it is not easily angered, it keeps no record of wrongs. Love does not delight in evil but rejoices with the truth. It always protects, always trusts, always hopes, always perseveres. Love never fails.*"
>
> (1 Corinthians 13:4-8a)

These verses are beautiful and true, yet at the same time almost impossible to live out in our own strength. If you want to live this way, but have no clue how, ask God to transform your heart, to help you see people through His loving eyes, and to allow His unending love for people to flow through you.

In closing, I would like to share the most important truth of all, in fact a truth that will give you the strength, power and love to show godly character in all situations.

It is the fact that God loves YOU.

> *"For I am convinced that neither death nor life, neither angels nor demons, neither the present nor the future, nor any powers, neither height nor depth, nor anything else in all creation, will be able to separate us from the love of God that is in Christ Jesus our Lord."*
>
> (Romans 8:38-39)

> *"And I pray that you, being rooted and established in love, may have power, together with all the Lord's holy people, to grasp how wide and long and high and deep is the love of Christ, and to know this love that surpasses knowledge — that you may be filled to the   measure of all the fullness of God."*
>
> (Ephesians 3:17b-19)

That is also my prayer for you.

Anita Elisabeth

Many people have supported me in my journey to publish this booklet. I could not possibly thank all those who contributed, but I would like to mention a few in particular.

I would like to thank my precious mother Sjoukje van den Brink-Rullmann, who always believes in me, always cheers me on, and used her incredible knowledge of languages to check the texts.

A big thank you to Joy Phillips and Gijs Dragt, for their professional contributions in creating the final version of this book. Many thanks to Marieke Fennema, who has the incredible gift of keeping me on target on the essentials. A thank you to Bob Phillips, who immediately supported me and believed in me in this process.

A thank you to all who helped me work through choosing the cover. A big thank you to Laura Olij for her dedicated work in supporting the publishing process.

Anita Elisabeth van den Brink
Amsterdam, Europe

The Bible verses quoted here are drawn primarily from the King James Version, from The Message, and from the New International Version, chosen based on which translation most clearly reflected the point I was making. I opted not to specify which version was used for each individual chapter and verse, since the additional distracted from the message of the text!

ISBN: 978-90-824092-0-8

www.ingramcontent.com/pod-product-compliance
Lightning Source LLC
Chambersburg PA
CBHW032102040426
42449CB00007B/1163